The Kids Book of
CANADIAN GEOGRAPHY

WRITTEN AND ILLUSTRATED BY

Briony Penn

KIDS CAN PRESS

This book is dedicated to Callum, Ronan, Brighde, Charlotte
and my excellent research assistant, Christie.

Acknowledgements

Dr. Phillip Dearden, Dept. of Geography, University of Victoria; Dr. Jean Brouard, Adjunct Prof. of Forestry Department,
University of Alberta; Dr. Sally John, Dr. Jim Monger, Dr. Robin June Hood, Elizabeth Woods-Buchanan,
Adrienne Mason, Jacky Booth, Donald Gunn, Malcolm Penn, Virginia Penn, Carolyn Zyha, Evelyn Hamilton.

Text and illustrations © 2008 Briony Penn

Kids Can Press gratefully acknowledges the financial support of the Government of Ontario,
through the Ontario Media Development Corporation; the Ontario Arts Council; the Canada Council
for the Arts; and the Government of Canada, through the CBF, for our publishing activity.

Published in Canada and the U.S. by Kids Can Press Ltd.
25 Dockside Drive, Toronto, ON M5A 0B5

Kids Can Press is a Corus Entertainment Inc. company

www.kidscanpress.com

Edited by Linda Biesenthal, Louise Oborne and Sheila Barry
Designed by Julia Naimska

Printed and bound in Altona, Manitoba, Canada, in 7/2016 by Friesens Corporation

CM 08 0 9 8 7 6 5 4 3 2

Library and Archives Canada Cataloguing in Publication

Penn, Briony
The kids book of Canadian geography / Briony Penn.

Includes index.
Target audience: For ages 8–12.
ISBN 978-1-55074-890-1

1. Canada—Geography—Juvenile literature. I. Title.

GB131.P46 2008   j917.1   C2007-906085-4

FSC
www.fsc.org
MIX
Paper from
responsible sources
FSC® C016245

CONTENTS

CANADA'S AMAZING GEOGRAPHY

Canada is the second biggest country in the world. That makes it an amazing place to study geography — the story of the earth. If you travelled from the Pacific to the Atlantic Ocean, and from our southern border to the Arctic Ocean, you could explore deep inlets, lush rain forests, towering mountains, raging rivers, dry grasslands, sparse tundra and even pocket deserts. In each of these places, landscape and life evolved, shaping one another into the geography of the Canada you know today.

Clues in the Landscape

The ever-changing story of Canada's geography — from earliest times on Earth until today — is told in its rocks, soils, plants and animals, including humans. Even your own backyard may hold clues of erupting volcanoes, ancient creatures, ice-age glaciers and incredible cultures. Everywhere in Canada, you can find traces of what shaped the land and how plants, animals and people have come and gone. Big rocks on a beach, fossils in a cliff, place names on a map, even the wildflowers growing in a vacant lot all have amazing stories to tell.

2. What can you tell from digging a hole in an Alberta farm field? That over thousands of years, rotting grasses and bison dung formed the rich, black soil the Prairies are famous for.

3. What can you tell when you can't dig a hole in the ground? That you are in the tundra, a place where the ground is permanently frozen and lemmings, woolly plants and lichens survive.

4. What do pillows of black rock tell you about Haida Gwaii (Queen Charlotte Islands)? That the islands formed when lava cooled after flowing out of an ancient volcano.

5. What does a huge rock in the middle of a plain tell you? That an ice sheet carried it hundreds of kilometres from the mountain it tumbled off.

1. Why do geographers look at rivers? Because they are great shapers of the landscape, carving deep valleys, level plains and places as spectacular as Niagara Falls.

6. What does a chorus of Pacific treefrogs tell you? That you are in a lush temperate rain forest with mild winters, wet summers and plenty of shady, freshwater swamps.

8. Why are fossils of tropical sea creatures found in the Rockies so interesting? Because they are clues that the mountains were once submerged reefs in an ancient, distant sea.

9. What does a ptarmigan tell you about the northern landscape? Ptarmigans grow feathers that are the colour of the tundra in the summer and the colour of snow for the rest of the year.

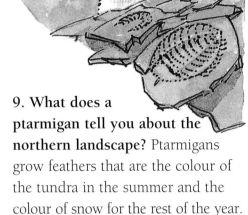

10. What do stone tools, shaped for spearing and cleaning fish, tell you about rivers in New Brunswick? That First Peoples lived along them thousands of years ago and relied on big runs of salmon to survive.

11. What do Heart's Content and Fortune Bay tell you about the coast of Newfoundland? That the fishermen who named them were safe in these harbours from the fierce winds and giant icebergs of the Atlantic Ocean.

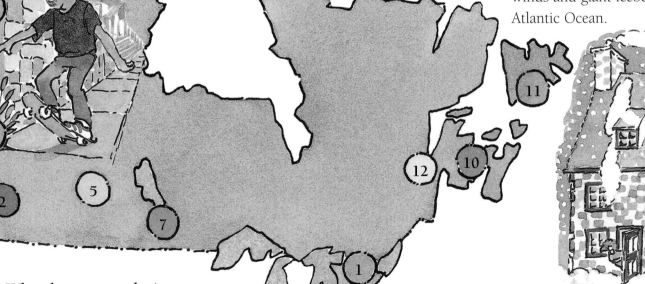

7. What does a water-loving willow bursting through a sidewalk in Winnipeg tell you? That the city was built on top of the Red River floodplain.

12. What do the steep roofs of old Quebec houses tell you? That settlers survived harsh, snowy winters by constructing buildings that would shed snow when it piled up.

CANADA IS BORN

Canada began as a single island about the size of Labrador. If you live near Great Slave Lake in the Northwest Territories, you are sitting on part of that first "super-island" formed by chains of erupting volcanoes that emerged out of the sea 4 billion years ago. Here you will find the oldest rocks in the world.

Island by island, Canada grew out from that core marking the beginning of the North American continent. If you time-travelled back 2 billion years, crossing Canada from sea to sea would have been a shorter trek than you would make today. You would have to go only from what is now Calgary to present-day Ottawa, but you would need mountain-climbing gear to scale the jagged peaks in between. The land that would become

British Columbia hadn't yet formed nor had much of Nunavut and the Maritimes. So just how did the continent Canadians call home grow to include all the places we know today? Scientists explain how through the theory of continent building.

Continent Building

The cooling of Earth makes continents move and grow. Heat escapes through cracks in the ocean floor and drives large plates of cooling oceanic crust over the mantle. The mantle is the layer of thick melted rock, or magma, between Earth's hard inner core and the crust. These plates of oceanic crust move continuously at about the speed your hair grows, carrying a lighter continental crust on top, like suitcases on an airport conveyor belt. The continental crust includes the rock of continents, islands and their reefs.

When plates pull apart, magma oozes between the plates and makes more oceanic crust. When plates slide past each other, earthquakes rumble. When plates carrying continental crust crash into each other, the oceanic crust is forced back down into the mantle. The continental crust stays on top and piles up into mountains, just like suitcases do at the end of a conveyor belt. This is what makes continents grow and shrink.

Canada's mountains are formed in several ways where plates collide at the edges of the continent. Super-islands and their reefs surf in on the plates then pile up like suitcases. Chains of volcanoes also form when oceanic crust is sucked under the plate and spewed up as magma.

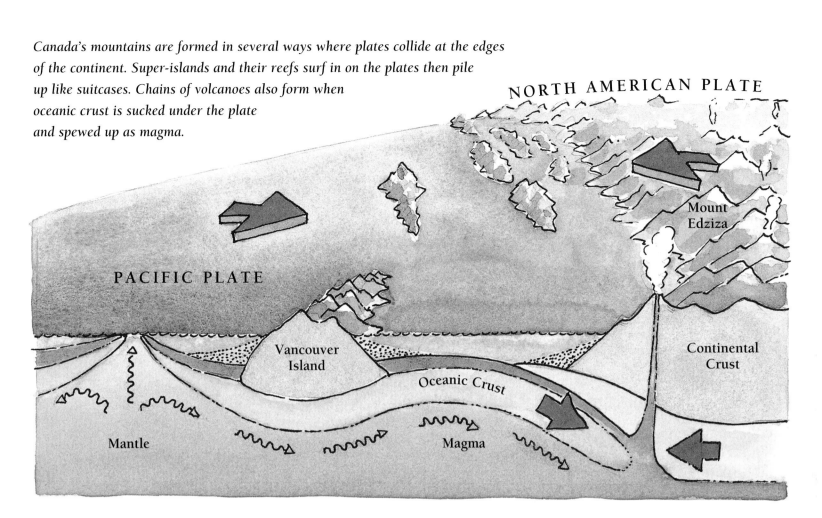

Mountains also form when the collision of plates causes the existing continental crust to buckle and fold.

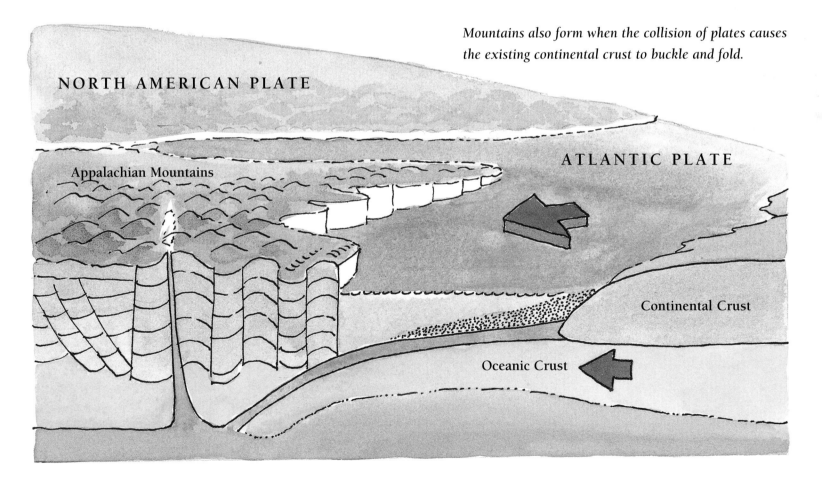

CANADA ON THE MOVE

Canada is a world traveller. The plate it sits on — the North American Plate — has carried Canada far and wide over the last 4 billion years. Canada has journeyed from the South Pole to the equator and now into the northern hemisphere. If you could live long enough on Earth, you could travel everywhere by continental drift and never move from your home.

Rodinia: 1 Billion Years Ago

A billion years ago, Earth's continental crust had grown into one big super-continent, Rodinia, lying over the South Pole. Antarctica and Australia were where the western provinces are now. And Ontario had a huge hole opening up in it as two plates pulled apart. This hole would eventually become the Great Lakes. About 750 million years ago, Rodinia began to break up into two huge continents — Gondwana and Laurentia.

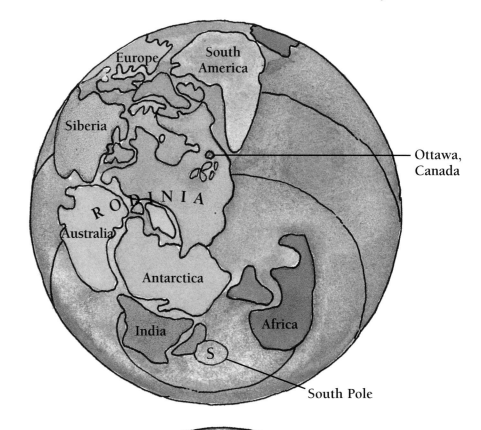

Laurentia: 600 Million Years Ago

Canada, except for the island of Newfoundland, was part of the continent of Laurentia that lay on the equator. The continent was still missing the Arctic, Atlantic and Pacific mountain ranges. But chains of volcanic islands, which would one day crash into the continent, were erupting in shallow seas inhabited by Earth's first creatures.

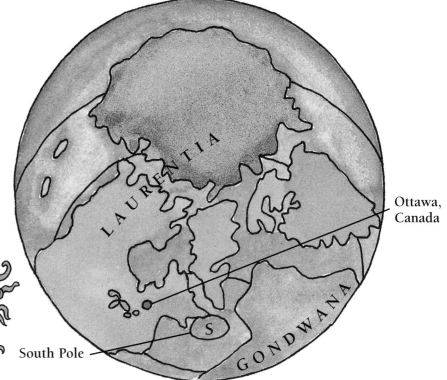

Pangea: 200 Million Years Ago

Over the next 400 million years, the continents drifted together again into a super-continent called Pangaea. If you could have looked out a window from Labrador, you would have seen Africa, not the Atlantic Ocean. As Africa squeezed in closer, old seabeds buckled up into the Appalachian Mountains. Greenland surfed in and crumpled up the super-islands of the north, forming the Arctic Mountains. The middle of Laurentia was a low plain. Shallow seas flooded in and out of what are now the Prairie provinces, creating reefs and swamps — not the best place for farming! When Pangaea was complete, early dinosaurs could walk across Canada, through Africa, and all the way to Australia without getting their feet wet.

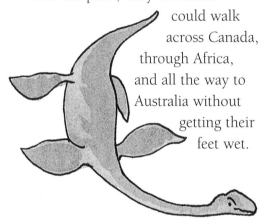

North America: 60 Million Years Ago

Over the next 140 million years, Pangaea broke back up into smaller continents. Canada headed west with the North American Plate. Africa moved east as the Atlantic Ocean opened up with the Atlantic Rift, except for a chunk that hitched a ride with Canada and became Newfoundland. On the west coast, the North American Plate plowed into a series of super-islands, each forming a different mountain range of the Western Cordillera. By 60 million years ago, Canada's landscape was beginning to look familiar.

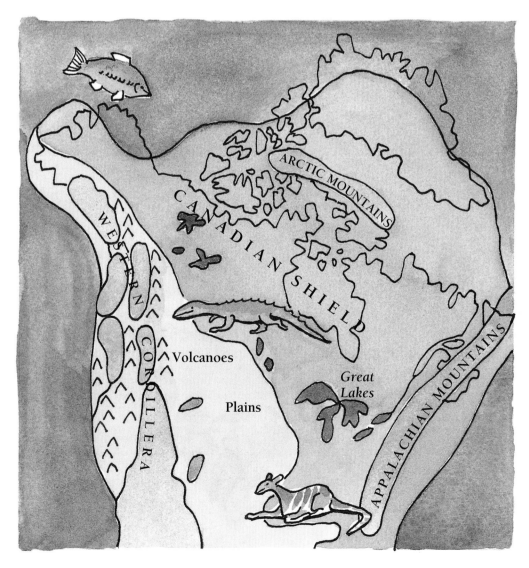

CANADA'S CLIMATE THEN AND NOW

Climate affects everything in the landscape — from how and where plants grow, to how and where animals and people live.

But Canada's climate has not always been like it is today. Clues from the past are preparing us for future climate change.

The Ancient Atmosphere

While continents grew and drifted around the globe, volcanoes poured carbon dioxide and water vapour into the atmosphere. Four billion years ago, Canada was like an overheated greenhouse with unbreathable air, far worse than any city smog. The arrival of plant life in the sea 3.5 billion years ago changed all that. Oceanic plants drew carbon dioxide out of the air and released oxygen into it. This made way for life both in the sea and on the land. As plants spread over Earth and its oceans, they pulled more and more carbon dioxide from the air, making the atmosphere cooler and more livable. The fresh Canadian air that we breathe today is thanks to our forests and oceans, which continue this amazing process.

Canada's Climate Evolves

By 60 million years ago, our continent had drifted roughly to where it is today, and Canada's climate began to evolve. The heat of the sun drove air masses and ocean currents around Earth and caused Canada to have hot and cold places and wet and dry places. The angle of the sun's rays also affected climate: the farther north, the more angled the sun's rays and the cooler the climate.

You can experience most of Canada's climates in one climb to the top of Mount Robson, in British Columbia.

Elevation is also important — the higher the mountains, the colder and drier the climate is.

Our Climate Today

Canada's three main climate zones are continental, maritime and polar. Canada is famous for its cold, snowy winters and hot, humid summers. This type of continental climate is typical for the interior of the country. Regions near oceans, that are slow to cool down and heat up, have more moderate maritime climates. The east and west coasts have milder winters, cooler summers and with all that water around there is more evaporation and rainfall. Where the ocean freezes in cold polar regions, there is less water for evaporation, and the climate is dry.

1. Windiest Place in Canada:
Cape St. James, Haida Gwaii (Queen Charlotte Islands), is windy 99 percent of the time, with wind speeds over 100 km/h (62 m.p.h.)

3. Wettest Place in Canada:
8123 mm (320 in.) precipitation in 1931, Henderson Lake, British Columbia

5. Driest Place in Canada:
130 mm (5 in.) precipitation a year, Resolute Bay, Cornwallis Island, Nunavut

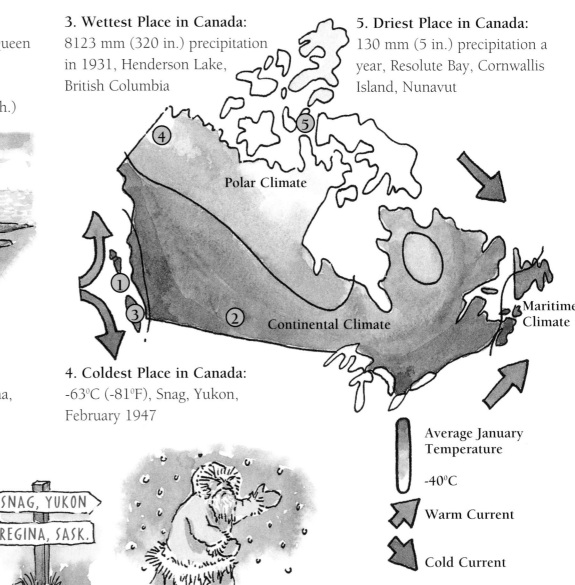

Polar Climate

Continental Climate

Maritime Climate

Average January Temperature

-40^0C

Warm Current

Cold Current

2. Hottest Place in Canada:
45^0C (113^0F) southeast of Regina, Saskatchewan, July 1937

4. Coldest Place in Canada:
-63^0C (-81^0F), Snag, Yukon, February 1947

SNAG, YUKON

REGINA, SASK.

Rain Shadows

Mountains are big climate shapers. Just as they cast shadows from the sun, they cast shadows from the rain. Rain shadows, such as the western prairie and Gulf of Georgia, receive smaller amounts of rainfall.

Weather and Climate

Daily temperatures and precipitation (such as rain and snow) give us our weather. Long-term weather patterns give us our climate. Weather changes rapidly, but climate changes more slowly.

Climate Change

By drilling down through ice, geographers have collected clues about climate over time. They have observed that climates warm up and cool down as air masses, ocean currents and carbon levels in the atmosphere change. Worldwide our climate is changing dramatically because we have released fossil fuels (oil, gas and coal) that raise carbon levels, which leads to increased temperatures. Clues of climate change include the melting of the permafrost (permanently frozen soils) in the Arctic, record droughts and more extreme weather events everywhere, such as heat waves, blizzards and tornadoes. Climate change is a huge threat to our way of life. Learning to read the landscape can help us to solve the problem of climate change.

Winds

Gulf of Georgia Rain Shadow

Western Prairie Rain Shadow

Vancouver Island

Western Cordillera

11

SHAPED BY SUN, WIND AND WATER

Imagine Saskatoon with huge, smouldering volcanoes and steep river valleys. That was the picture billions of years ago. What changed the landscape from towering mountains to the flat prairie you see today? Sun, wind and water — the forces of erosion.

Wind and water (in the form of ice and rain) wear down mountains. Glaciers scrape the land clear. And heat from the sun causes rocks to shatter. These changes in the landscape happen very slowly over millions of years. But other changes, such as mudslides caused by torrential rains, happen suddenly.

Soil in the Making

Soil begins to form when rocks are ground into tiny grains of sand and clay — a process called weathering. Sun, wind, rain, rivers and ice break down rock and carry its sediments to the lowlands and the coast. Here these sediments mix with the remains of decayed plants and animals and, over time, soil forms. Without sediments, we would have no soil. And without soil, Canada would have no trees, plants or animals, including us.

Sedimentary Wonders

Without erosion, we also wouldn't have sedimentary rock — the rock on which many Canadian cities are built. Sedimentary rock forms when sediments such as sand, mud or clay pile up on top of each other year after year. Then, under great pressure, they cement into rock.

Interesting places can form where sediments build up. The Prairies formed from sedimentary rock. So did the Grand Banks. The once plentiful cod would never have thrived off the shores of Newfoundland and Labrador if erosion hadn't deposited sediments to build the shallow shelf of the Grand Banks. Here the warmer waters teemed with plankton and smaller fish — an abundant food source for the cod.

Clues in the Hoodoos

Outlaws used to hide in the hoodoos of Drumheller Valley, Alberta. Wind and water sculpted these amazing rock formations by breaking down the layers of sedimentary rock at different rates. Wandering around the gullies, you can decode the history of the Badlands just by looking at a hoodoo's layers. Harder rocks, such as limestone (old sea reefs), take longer to erode while mudstone (old lake beds) and sandstone (old beaches) wear down more quickly.

Erosion in Action

While continents build at the edges of plates, erosion grinds them down. Erosion is responsible for flattening the Canadian Shield. Even the Rockies and Laurentians will one day erode away to nothing.

Imagine you could watch a time-lapse video made over millions of years from the top of Mount Waddington in the Coast Mountains. You'd see the action of the sun, wind, ice and water eroding one of British Columbia's tallest mountains. You'd see the rock shattering from extreme heat and cold. Then ferocious winds would blow it away. Tumbling water would grind these rocks into tiny grains. And some of the runoff from melting glaciers would reach the Fraser River. Someday, these grains might end up as sand between the toes of people strolling the beaches of Vancouver.

CARVED BY ICE

About 800 million years ago, the first ice age set in. Since then, ice ages have come and gone. The last ice age was at its peak in Canada just 17 000 years ago. At that time, two massive ice sheets covered almost the whole country. The ice was so thick that it would have buried the Parliament Buildings in Ottawa ten times over. As the glaciers — those powerful agents of erosion — inched forward, they scraped rocks, trees and soil off the landscape and ground them into bits. The enormous weight of the ice squished the land, and shorelines bounced up and down like yo-yos. As the ice melted and the glaciers retreated, the land bounced back, rivers reversed directions and new lakes appeared and disappeared, sometimes overnight. Today, you can find ice-age clues of these features carved in the landscape, evidence of the tremendous power of ancient glaciers.

Trails of the Glaciers

1. Glaciers move because their enormous weight melts the ice underneath them and slowly slides them downhill. As they inch along, they carry ground-up bits of the landscape, called till.

2. Like giant bulldozers, glaciers gouge out river valleys and transform places. Thanks to glaciers, elk can graze in fertile U-shaped valleys.

3. Till that is pushed in front of or along the sides of a glacier is called moraine.

4. Glaciers pick up rocks and carry them great distances. Bump into a big unusual rock, or erratic, that looks out of place and you've discovered another clue of a glacier passing by.

5. Check out scratch marks left on rock faces and you can tell which direction a glacier moved.

Sea Levels and Shorelines

First Nations kids on the West Coast learn flood stories from their elders, since many ancient villages sunk underwater like the lost city of Atlantis when the glaciers melted. Haida Gwaii (Queen Charlotte Islands) bounced up and down over the last 20 000 years. As the ice sheets formed, sea levels fell. When they melted, sea levels rose. At the same time, the changing weight of the ice sheets caused continental crust to bounce up and down on Earth's mantle. This bouncing effect is similar to what happens when you sit on a balloon: one spot pushes in and another spot pops out. Places such as Vancouver Island got pushed down by the ice, while Haida Gwaii popped up as much as 100 m (328 ft.), before sinking again.

Changing Shorelines

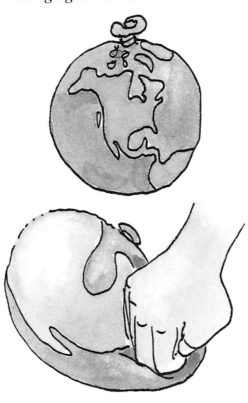

During the ice age, shorelines were pushed up out of the water from the weight of the ice. A huge amount of water was locked up in the icesheets, dropping the sea levels.

Ice-Age Oases

When you clean pots and pans with a big scrubber, you often miss a few places. The same is true of the glaciers scouring the land. There were a few places in Canada that the ice sheets missed. These special places are called refugia because they harbour the plants, animals and perhaps humans that took refuge until the glaciers melted. Some were small edges of coastline, such as Brooks Peninsula on Vancouver Island. Some were high mountain peaks, such as Barbeau Peak on Ellesmere Island, Nunavut. Beringia was a huge plain between Yukon and Siberia where it was too dry for glaciers to form. During the last ice age, Beringia supported herds of ice-age animals on its plains and maybe even the humans that hunted them.

EVIDENCE OF ANCIENT LIFE

While Canada drifted around from hemisphere to hemisphere, collecting and shedding continental crust, animals and plants drifted with the land, slowly evolving as they went. This is what makes Canada's fossil record so interesting: it tells the story of creatures from all over the globe that lived at different times. Spend some time looking at sedimentary rocks and you can see evidence of this ancient life in the fossil record.

Canada's oldest fossils are carpets of algae found in the Canadian Shield, dating back 2 billion years. Canada's oddest fossil may be 7 kg (15 lb.) of dinosaur dung (known as coprolite), dropped by a Tyrannosaurus rex near Eastend, Saskatchewan, about 75 million years ago.

Fossil Forests of Joggins

Near Joggins, Nova Scotia, a fossil forest pokes out of a cliff that has been worn away by huge tides in the Bay of Fundy. The forest dates back more than 300 million years, when Nova Scotia was an island close to the equator, and ancient plants flourished in its hot, swampy environment.

The trees were giant club mosses and horsetails 30 m (98 ft.) high with thick, scaly trunks. Huge ferns spread out under their dense foliage. On the forest floor, leafy vines twined around fallen trunks. All these lush plants sheltered fist-sized cockroaches, huge scorpions and dragonflies and ancient amphibians. In 1851, the skeleton of the first

reptile was discovered in the stump of a fossilized tree.

Forests such as the one near Joggins are sometimes called coal forests. When the giant trees died and toppled into the swamps, they were buried and slowly compressed, forming coal after millions of years.

ANCIENT TIMELINE

4.6 billion years ago:	4 billion years ago:	3.5 billion years ago:
Earth forms out of dust cloud.	Volcanic eruption starts creating the North American continent.	Primitive life forms (bacteria and algae) appear.

Dinosaur Graveyard

One of the world's largest dinosaur graveyards is in Dinosaur Provincial Park in southern Alberta. Fossilized skulls, leg bones, whole skeletons, pieces of skin and eggs from 40 different kinds of dinosaurs have been excavated in the park.

Dinosaurs roamed this part of Alberta 75 million years ago. In those days, the Prairies were swampy lagoons with a tropical climate. Albertosaurus and Tyrannosaurus rex stalked plant-eating dinosaurs along the Red Deer River. Duck-billed Corythosaurus feasted on lush ferns along the riverbanks. Horned Centrosaurus chomped reeds and cattails in the swamps.

Creatures of the Burgess Shale

Canada's most spectacular fossil find was made in 1909 at Mount Burgess in the Rockies. Here scientists uncovered fossils of thousands of ancient sea creatures in shale (a type of sedimentary rock) at the top of the mountain. This great diversity of animals included sponges, sea worms and the first animals that developed eyes, mouths, guts, gills, pincers, jointed legs, shells and backbones. These creatures thrived along the muddy banks of a shallow sea surrounding a super-island in the South Pacific 530 million years ago. They died in a mudslide, trapped at the bottom of the sea. Three hundred million years later, they resurfaced, preserved in rock, 2500 m (8200 ft.) above sea level and thousands of kilometres from where they once swam. Some scientists say that the whole animal kingdom, including humans, can trace its ancestry back to the creatures of the Burgess Shale. It is one of the most important scientific sites in the world!

800 million years ago:	248 million years ago:	60 million years ago:
First ice age occurs.	Dinosaurs roam into Canada.	The outline of Canada begins to look like it does now, and dinosaurs have been extinct for 5 million years.

EVOLVING ECOSYSTEMS

When the last ice age ended 10 000 years ago, plants and animals slowly returned to the scraped, barren land from ice-free areas such as Beringia. Lichens and sedges from the tundra moved in first, followed by aspen, birch and willow trees. Ice-age animals such as woolly mammoths, mastodons and big-horned bison browsed on these pioneer plants. Sabre-tooth tigers and short-faced bears stalked the giant grazers.

As the climate gradually warmed, plant species from the ice-free lands to the south began to reappear. Birds and rodents carried spruce cones from areas that had escaped the ice sheets and turned tundra into boreal forest. Seeds of oaks, ashes and other deciduous woodland plants were carried north in the stomachs of birds and rooted in warm, wet spots. Winds blew grassland seeds onto the dry plains, and slowly the rich soils of the Prairies formed. Lush coastal rain forests spread up western valleys as decaying trees built up soil.

1. Coastal Rain Forest

Western hemlock, redcedars and Sitka spruce spread from island refugias along the rainy edge of the continent. Deer, elk and bears roamed the forest, and orcas followed salmon up the ice-carved fjords. Douglas-fir grew as high as 30-storey skyscrapers.

2. Western Cordillera

Tundra plants survived the ice on tops of mountains. Marmots relied on the alpine flowers, and golden eagles hunted the marmots. Boreal forest took root on the upper mountain slopes and in rain forests on the lower slopes.

3. Tundra

Treeless tundra moved onto the land once the ice had melted. Only tiny lichens and sedges took hold on the permafrost. Barren-ground caribou grazed on lichens, while predators such as wolves followed the caribou.

4. Laurentian Woodlands

Laurentian woodlands on the southeast edge of the Canadian Shield grew out of old muddy riverbeds and seabed. Ice-age grazers and flocks of passenger pigeons carried seeds of maple, ash and oak trees up from the south.

5. Boreal Forest

Willow, aspen and birch seeds blew in the wind and skated over the ice. Clumps of black and white spruce rooted in the small pockets of till left by the glaciers. Muskeg, thick with insects and sphagnum moss, developed in the poorly drained places. Broad-hooved moose browsed in the muskeg, attracting predators such as wolves.

6. Prairie

Grasslands formed on the dry plains. Wheatgrass, bluestem grass and goldenrod blew up from the south. Aspen parklands grew at the edges of the prairie. Pocket gophers and badgers burrowed under the prairie. Bison and pronghorn antelope grazed on top.

What Is an Ecosystem?

It took thousands of years for Canada's ecosystems to evolve into what they are today — particular communities of plants, animals and people, and the climate, soils and landforms they live in. An ecosystem can apply to whatever chunk of the world a geographer wants to study — from biomes (a large ecological region characterized by similar vegetation, climate and living organisms within it) the size of continents, to ecoregions the size of provinces, right down to mini-ecosystems such as swamps. To decode your landscape, it helps to know something about how your regional ecosystem evolved.

7. Acadian Woodlands

Woodland and ocean species met at the eastern edge of the continent. Walnut trees and pitcher plants from the south took root. Northern spruce, pine and balsam fir mixed with the hardwoods. Cod, salmon and humpback whales fed on the rich plankton offshore.

8. Carolinian Woodlands

Tulip trees, spice bushes, snakes and songbirds arrived from the far south as the climate warmed. Beech and oak trees flourished in the rich mud of an ancient glacial lake bed.

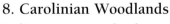

FIRST PEOPLES

I f you live around Old Crow, Yukon, you could visit one of the earliest-known human camps in Canada. The discovery of spear tips near some mammoth bones in the Bluefish Caves is a clue to the arrival of humans in the north. There are many theories about where people came from.

We know that the very First Peoples had at least stone tools and fire to shape the landscape for their needs. By 11 000 years ago, many large ice-age mammals, such as mammoths, had become extinct. Hunters turned to bison, deer and sea mammals, using small spear tips. As the glaciers retreated further, family groups travelled along rivers and shorelines in search of food. As the climate warmed and plants and animals spread, people followed them. Populations grew, trading networks evolved and humans started leaving more clues of their lives on the land, such as carved stones, hunting fences and settlements. The most enduring clues to the past are in the First Nation's oral traditions and stories.

Hunters may have come over the Beringia land bridge over 13 500 years ago or followed the ice-age mammals up from the south. There are also clues that they came from the west by boat along the ice-free parts of the coastline maybe as early as 15 000 years ago.

Each ecosystem shaped a unique way of life and culture. Each culture has its own language to describe local plants, animals and geography. There are 12 language families that share almost the same borders as Canada's regional ecosystems.

1. People of the Tundra

Inuktitut-speaking people have traditionally followed the caribou, fished and hunted sea mammals.

The clues to their way of life are in the Inukshuks and stone fences that proved to be the best way to herd and catch caribou. They used ice for winter shelters and caribou skins for summer tents.

2. People of the Boreal Forest

Athabaskan-speaking people moved into the western boreal forest, and Algonkian-speaking people moved into the eastern boreal forest. Traditionally people had seasonal camps because game such as caribou and moose move with the seasons. So few clues are left to mark their passage through the land.

Firepits, bones of animals, and stone tools found in the soil are the only clues.

3. People of the Laurentian and Carolinian Woodlands

In the warm climate and on the rich soils, Iroquoian-speaking people, the Haudenosaunee, farmed and built villages. Their longhouses stood on shorelines beside fields of corn. They travelled the rivers in birchbark canoes. Today, you can still see their long, curved burial mounds.

4. People of the Coastal Rain Forest

Isolated islands and rugged coastlines helped shape unique coastal cultures from the Salish in the south to the Haida and Tlingit in the north. They have all depended on the abundant salmon, shellfish and marine mammals of the rich coastal ecosystem to survive. Carvings of these animals are found on everything from totem poles to tools. You can still see the stone traps they used to catch salmon.

5. People of the Western Cordillera

In the mountains, the interior Salish- and Kutenai-speaking people have hunted deer and elk, gathered root crops and berries and fished the rivers. In winter, they traditionally lived in pit houses dug into gravel terraces, the remains of which you can still see today. In summer, the Kutenai speakers travelled to the prairie with mat houses (teepees made of reeds).

6. People of the Prairie

The Siouan-speaking people, and later the Algonkian-speaking people, relied on the bison herds that roamed the plains. Hunters caught bison in traps or drove them off coulees, ravines washed out by glacial floods. Prairie peoples left stone circles and butchering sites where bison bones still lie.

7. People of the Acadian Woodlands

The Beothuk-speaking people of Newfoundland and the maritime Algonkian-speaking people traditionally built fish traps in estuaries, gathered plants and harvested marine mammals and shellfish from the sea. Today, you can still see evidence of the stone traps.

Fire and the Canadian Landscape

If you could time-travel back 500 years, you would find the skies full of smoke every autumn on the prairie. Fire recycles nutrients back into the soil. First Peoples lit fires to maintain grasslands for grazing animals and the gathering of roots and berries. When European settlers stopped the burning, many of these plants and animals started to disappear. Trees started to grow where grasslands had been, and grazing in the spring wasn't as good for the large herds of animals.

NEW ARRIVALS ON CANADA'S SHORES

A new wave of people arrived on the continent as long ago as 1000 years. European explorers and traders came in small numbers at first, but the germs and guns that they brought had a devastating effect. Ninety percent of First Peoples died from diseases these newcomers carried. Canada was viewed as a place of vast riches. But in a short period of time, its wealth was plundered as whales, beavers, otters and bison were hunted almost to extinction. With changes in the way of life of both aboriginal people and the bison and beavers they relied on, Canada became a very different place.

From the 1500s on, settlers from Europe and Asia arrived on Canada's shores with dreams of starting new lives. They built farms and towns that looked like the places they had left. And they brought the animals and plants with which they were familiar. Some species, such as the purple loosestrife plants, starlings and rats, became unruly pests that drastically changed ecosystems.

Atlantic puffin looking down on Basque whaling station on Labrador coast.

Whales, Fish and Furs

Place names such as Whaling Station Bay, British Columbia, and Blackfish Cove, Newfoundland, are clues to an industry that started 1000 years ago. The Vikings, who were whalers, left the remains of a settlement at L'Anse aux Meadows in AD 1000. About 500 years later, European whalers started hunting bowhead whales off the East Coast. The arrival of Captain Cook in 1778 on the West Coast, led to the start of the sea otter fur trade. When whales and sea otters were pushed to near extinction, traders looked to other species such as the cod, herring and salmon. Walk along inlets on either coast and you can find remains of old fish canneries. When beaver hats became fashionable in Europe, fur traders built forts such as Fort Garry (now Winnipeg) along traditional paddle routes of major rivers. As demands for hats grew and beavers were hunted out, trade routes pushed farther and farther west into the wetlands of Canada. A way of life was changing rapidly.

Golden eagle looking down on Fort Nelson (York Factory) at Hudson Bay.

Farms and Settlements

Farming settlements grew up on the shorelines close to where Europeans first landed, such as Montreal and Halifax. Farms and towns spread south and west down rivers and lakes. Settlers cleared forests and fought locusts, fire, floods and drought to grow their crops. First nations lost much of their best lands to European settlement. The original ecosystems of southern Canada from coast to coast had largely disappeared by the 1900s. If you walk in the tall-grass prairie preserve of Winnipeg's Living Prairie Museum, or the Carolinian woodland at Point Pelee in Ontario, you can experience what it was like before Europeans arrived. As the country opened up and transportation routes grew, settlers made long journeys to settle on the Prairies and along the West Coast.

Mines and Timber

Prospectors the world over were lured by dreams of striking it rich. From Dawson City, Yukon, to Labrador, miners looked first for gold, then silver, nickel, copper and other minerals. Prospecting lines, mines and railway spurs criss-crossed the landscape. By the early 1900s, Canada's wood and paper was in demand all over the world. Lumberjacks worked for companies clearing valley bottoms of the biggest trees, from British Columbia to Newfoundland and Labrador. As demand rose, they went after the smaller timber in more remote areas, such as the northern boreal forest and western mountains.

Canada in the Twentieth Century

Many Canadian kids have relatives who came to Canada in the early twentieth century. Wherever railways and roads were built, people travelled on them to find jobs and resources. Many moved west, while others stayed in eastern cities to work in factories. Minerals and wood were shipped to factories where people made everything from trains to zippers. Steel, paper and chemical factories spread around the Great Lakes. Most of Canada's 35 million people now live in suburbs along our border with the United States. Not since the last ice age has there been such a huge change to the landscape.

TUNDRA

The tundra ecosystem lies north of the Arctic Circle. Tundra is vast, treeless, rocky land and bogs carpeted with lichens and mosses. It lies on the northern edge of the Canadian Shield.

The Ancient Landscape

In ancient times, volcanoes and old seabeds squished up like accordions, creating the mountainous islands of the north. The southern arctic coastal plain flooded and drained as sea levels changed, building up layers of sandstone rich with fossils. Ice-age glaciers bulldozed everything and flattened the coastal plains. Frost shattered majestic mountains and sent boulders plummeting to the sea.

ARCTIC OCEAN

ELLESMERE ISLAND

QUEEN ELIZABETH ISLANDS

Resolute

NORTHWEST TERRITORIES

VICTORIA ISLAND

treeline

Arctic Circle

NUNAVUT

HUDSON BAY

Climate

The polar climate has changed over time, but it has always been harsh. During mid-winter in Iqaluit, the three hours of daylight rarely warm the air above -25 degrees C. Freezing and thawing of the ground have created ice wedges, stripes and blister-like hills, called pingos. Climate change is melting the permafrost that has been frozen since the last ice age, causing mudslides.

How a pingo forms

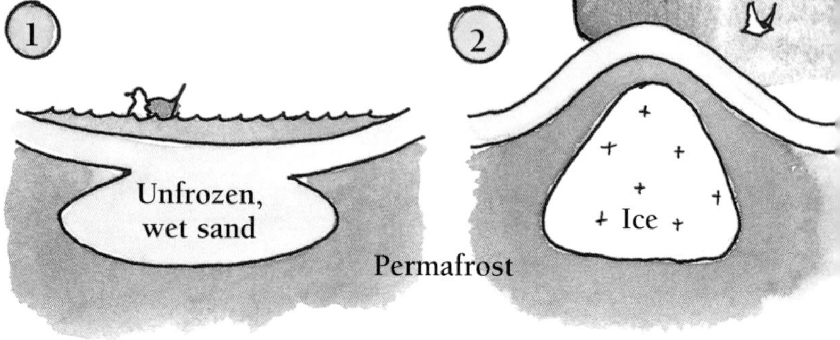

① Unfrozen, wet sand
Permafrost

② + Ice +

Plants and Animals

Tundra was the first ecosystem to develop as the ice melted. With permafrost, nothing decayed quickly so soils developed very slowly. Only the hardiest lichens pioneered the rock deserts of the northern islands. Slowly, soils built up in the coastal plains and flowering plants took root. Caribou, muskox and Arctic hare moved in to browse on sedges and lichens.

In summer, half the bird species of Canada migrate to the bogs and feed on clouds of insects. Resident snowy owls keep down the lemming population, and gyrfalcons hunt ptarmigan. Arctic currents churn up nutrients in undersea troughs — the feeding grounds for copepods (small crustaceans). Arctic cod and bowhead whales feed on the copepods. Belugas, narwhals, walrus and seabirds feed on the larger krill. Arctic char run up the rivers in late summer. Polar bears ride the sea ice looking for seals. Climate change is having a huge impact on arctic animals.

First Peoples

During the ice age, small groups of people travelled from Beringia and later spread out to the eastern islands. Here their 4000-year-old stone arrows have been found. The Paleo-Eskimos had no dogs or sleds and lived in small skin houses encircled by stones, which still lie on the landscape. The Dorset people built snow houses and caught caribou using stone fences and Inukshuks. About 500 years ago, the Thule people, ancestors of the modern Inuit, arrived from the west and brought the first kayaks and dogsleds for hunting sea mammals.

Auyuittuq National Park

BAFFIN ISLAND

Iqaluit

QUEBEC

New Arrivals

In 1001, Leif Ericsson left Greenland and briefly landed at Baffin Island looking for a place to settle. About 500 years later, Martin Frobisher landed near the same spot. He didn't find the Northwest Passage he was looking for, but he thought he'd found gold — the trenches he dug are still there. He was followed by other explorers, whalers and traders who harvested narwhal tusks, sea mammal furs and oil from bowhead whales. Their bones still lie on the land. After Henry Hudson named Hudson Bay, more adventurers travelled the Arctic erecting monuments or grave cairns. World War II brought soldiers who built surveillance stations and prospectors looking for uranium, oil and gas.

Surveillance station on Victoria Island, built during the Cold War of the 1950s.

The Landscape Today

The tundra is probably the least changed landscape in Canada, but oil, gas and mining activities have left networks of roads, exploration corridors and pipelines crisscrossing the landscape, which alter traditional migration routes of wildlife. Open sea fishing and whale hunting are less common. Some Inuit families still take their tents and oil stoves

out onto the tundra to set up fishing and hunting camps during the spring. But bowhead whalebones that were once used for tent poles are more likely to be found in museums. Today, you can trek where only the Inuit travelled by following a 100 km (62 mi.) hiking trail through Pangnirtung Pass in Auyuittuq National Park.

Because the polar ice cap is melting, the North Pole is increasingly ice-free. Some scientists think that the fabled Northwest Passage may even open up for shipping traffic soon.

Dragonflies and robins now make their homes on the melting permafrost. The Inuit don't even have names for these newcomers in their language. The stone Inukshuks that marked the old caribou trails are now the symbol for the new territory of Nunavut and appear on Nunavut's flag.

Scientists fear the polar bear may go extinct because of climate change.

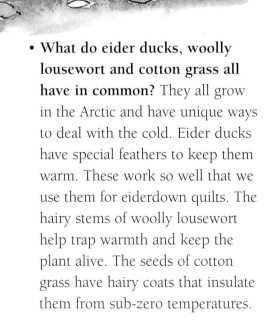

• **What do caribou antlers in the yards of most homes tell you about living in Nain, Labrador?** That hunting for food is still a way of life on the tundra. Most of the people who live in Nain are Inuit. They keep their snowmobiles and komatiks (wooden sleds) ready for caribou and fox hunts. The largest caribou herd in the world (up to 350 000 animals) passes near Nain as the caribou migrate north to their spring calving grounds.

• **What takes a minute to create and centuries to repair in the Arctic?** Vehicle tracks and garbage dumps. The tundra is a very fragile ecosystem. It takes centuries for just a tiny community of lichens and small plants to get a foothold because of the very short growing season. One bulldozer can set the tundra back as far as the ice ages. And garbage can sit on the tundra for eons without rotting.

• **What do eider ducks, woolly lousewort and cotton grass all have in common?** They all grow in the Arctic and have unique ways to deal with the cold. Eider ducks have special feathers to keep them warm. These work so well that we use them for eiderdown quilts. The hairy stems of woolly lousewort help trap warmth and keep the plant alive. The seeds of cotton grass have hairy coats that insulate them from sub-zero temperatures.

27

BOREAL FOREST

The vast ecosystem of the boreal forest covers half of Canada and spreads over the Canadian Shield. Here wetlands are linked by forests of spruce and aspen that give way to carpets of lichen in the north. In the west is a rolling terrain of spruce trees, barrens and wetlands. In the centre, around Hudson Bay, lies a belt of lakes and bogs. To the east, in northern Quebec and Labrador, you'll find forests, rivers and rocky ocean shores.

The Ancient Landscape

The boreal forest lies on the ancient core of the continent. Two hundred million years ago, volcanoes sprang up like castles as Africa crashed into Newfoundland and Greenland slammed into Labrador. As crust collected at the edges of the growing continent, minerals such as gold, silver, copper and nickel formed in the seams of melting rock.

Glaciers scraped much of this landscape down to bare rock. As the weight of the ice lifted, the landscape kept the shape of a teacup saucer. The depression in the saucer filled up with meltwaters, forming Hudson Bay. Smaller depressions elsewhere filled up with freshwater.

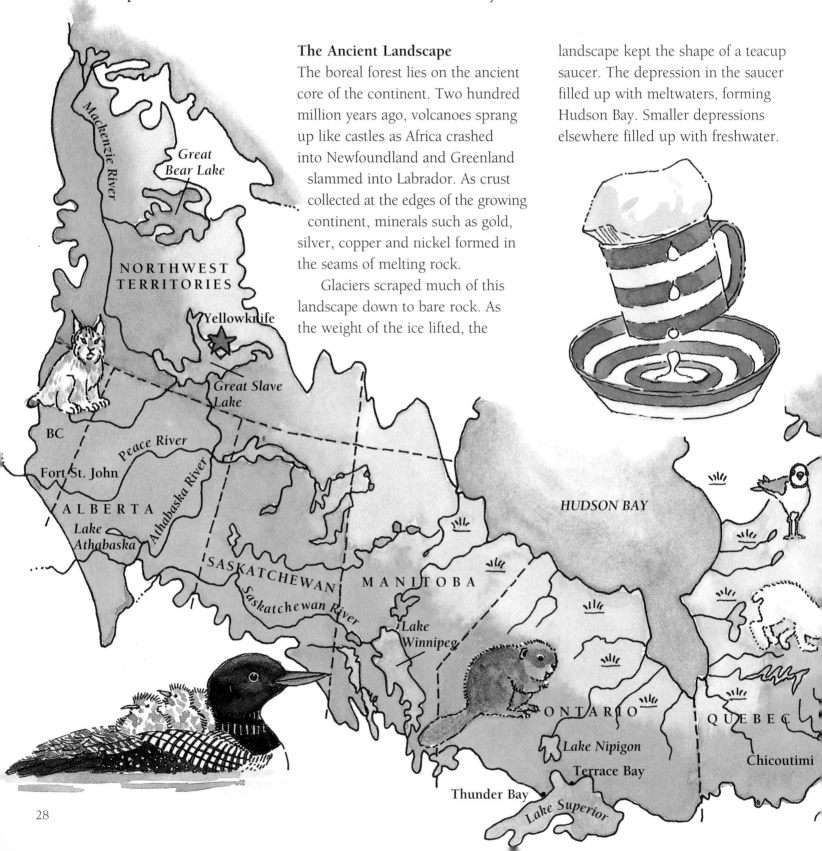

Mackenzie River

Great Bear Lake

NORTHWEST TERRITORIES

Yellowknife

Great Slave Lake

BC

Fort St. John

Peace River

ALBERTA

Lake Athabaska

Athabaska River

SASKATCHEWAN

Saskatchewan River

MANITOBA

Lake Winnipeg

HUDSON BAY

ONTARIO

Lake Nipigon

Terrace Bay

Thunder Bay

Lake Superior

QUEBEC

Chicoutimi

Climate

The west has a dry continental climate because it is far from the influence of the sea. With warm summers, forests reach as far north as the Mackenzie River delta. In the central region, winters are colder. The effects of the Great Lakes and Hudson Bay make it snowier. The Labrador Current drags cold weather over the eastern part of the boreal forest. In the summer, when the cold sea meets the warmer land, dense fog blocks out the sun. As climate changes, the boreal forest is predicted to change the most of all ecosystems.

Plants and Animals

As the glaciers melted, sphagnum moss filled spots where drainage was poor, forming bogs and muskeg. Anywhere that wasn't too wet, black and white spruce, jackpine and birch took root as seeds blew in from southern refugia. Today, broadhooved moose graze on willows and reeds in the wetlands. Wolves, bears, lynx and woodland caribou live in the forests. Lichens falling out of trees provide winter food for caribou. Bears browse sedges and roots in the spring and fish the rivers for chum salmon in the fall. Millions of birds migrate each spring to the wetlands and feed on the plentiful mosquitoes and blackfly.

When the Labrador Current started to flow, krill and other plankton thrived on the nutrients that floated up. Now, minke and blue whales feed on the krill, alongside huge schools of capelin. Harbour seals, harp seals and belugas feast on the fish. Guillemots, glaucous gulls and gannets breed on the cliffs. Arctic char and Atlantic salmon run up rivers in late summer.

How a bog forms

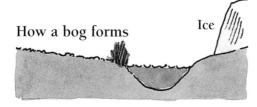

Ice

Spaghnum moss

Voisey's Bay

Goose Bay

LABRADOR

☐ Boreal

☐ Boreal Tundra

First Peoples

In the west, Athabaskan-speaking people depended on woodland caribou and moose for clothes, food and shelter. In winter, they wore snowshoes to hunt and built sturdy homes insulated with moss and bark. In summer, they travelled by foot or hide boats and lived in hide tents, harvesting berries and roots. In the central area, the Algonkian-speaking people were constantly on the move in their birchbark canoes looking for food. Rich fishing enabled the Ojibway to live in more permanent villages along the northern shores of Lake Superior. In the east, the Algonkian ancestors of the Innu, and the Thule people, ancestors of the Inuktitut-speaking peoples, met in the wide zone between tundra and forest. The Innu used spruce for lodges, birchbark for canoes and hides for warmth. Today, Inuit people still occupy the tundra, and Innu live in the boreal forests.

The Landscape Today

Canada's boreal forest is the largest expanse of boreal forest left in the world. A century of logging, mining, air pollution and acid rain has damaged the eastern boreal forest and acidified the lakes, but much still remains. Oil and gas exploration, logging, highways, mines and climate change are transforming all the landscape and traditional aboriginal ways of life. In the interior plateaus of the eastern area, nickel and iron have been discovered, and mining companies are building settlements, such as Voisey's Bay in Labrador.

New Arrivals

For five centuries, nations battled over fishing grounds for whales and cod, leaving only whalebones and small settlements on the northern coast. Fur traders set their sights on the beaver-rich wetlands draining into Hudson Bay, starting in 1670. The Hudson's Bay Company took over the area, and the beaver was hunted for 200 years. By the 1850s, fur traders had set up forts all the way to Fort Selkirk.

Prospectors started to discover rich deposits of copper, nickel and other minerals in the Canadian Shield, which brought mines, mining communities and roads into the region.

The trees of the boreal forest were the next valuable resource to harvest. Sawmills and pulp mills popped up as railways connected them to markets. Rivers were dammed for hydroelectricity to provide energy for mills. Company resource towns were built rapidly to house workers.

• **What makes white and black spruce trees so well adapted to the snowy, cold landscape of the north?** With their short, sloping branches that shed loads of snow easily, these two types of spruce trees are designed for long winters. If they had long branches such as redcedar in the rain forest, the branches would snap off under the weight of heavy snow and ice.

• **Where will you find paper, power and pickup trucks in the boreal forest?** From Fort St. John, British Columbia, to Terrace Bay, Ontario, and Chicoutimi, Quebec. Company towns were established in these places to harvest timber and process it into lumber and paper using the hydroelectric power of northern rivers. Company towns have mills, dams and housing for the workers. Many workers drive pickup trucks to work and keep snowmobiles and boats for hunting in their spare time.

• **Who made the boreal forest famous in his paintings?** Tom Thomson, who sometimes worked as a guide in Algonquin Park and was one of the Group of Seven artists. Here he captured the beauty of the boreal forest with his brush. At the beginning of the twentieth century, people were more interested in European landscapes than Canadian, until they saw their rugged beauty through Thomson's eyes. He drowned in Canoe Lake in 1917.

• **What makes grooves in the boreal forest rock other than glaciers?** Between Great Slave Lake and Great Bear Lake is a bare rock with a worn-down groove that is called Hoodoodzoo. Kids slid down the rock for thousands of years for fun as they travelled through. The Dogrib people believe that if you slide down without turning around you will live a long life.

LAURENTIAN WOODLANDS

The Laurentian woodlands ecosystem is a lowland area that includes the shorelines of the Great Lakes and the St. Lawrence River.

The Ancient Landscape

For 500 million years, water covered this region and buried the Canadian Shield under beds of sand and mud. About 100 million years ago, the sea floor cracked open and a necklace of volcanoes bubbled up. When the ice-age glaciers melted, the Champlain Sea flooded the lowlands once again. Belugas and sea lions could swim all the way to what is now Ottawa and volcanoes became islands in a sea. Then the lowlands bounced back up, thick with mud. Today, the St. Lawrence River cuts its way through this mud to the sea. There are over 1 million lakes and rivers in the low-lying woodlands.

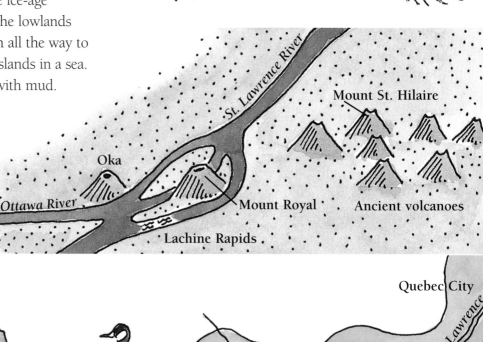

Climate

Most of the woodlands have warm, humid summers and large buildups of snow in the winter. Farther east along the St. Lawrence, wet summer squalls and fogs roll in from the sea, keeping the summers cooler.

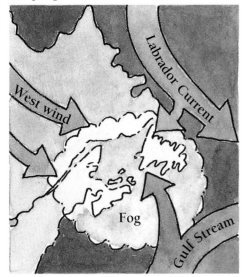

Plants and Animals

Thick canopies of oak, beech, hickory and ash trees grew up in the deep mud of the St. Lawrence lowlands. Where freshwater and salt water mixed, river fish such as sturgeon swam with belugas and other ocean mammals. The lush marshes became flyways for geese and ducks and corridors for otters and amphibians. Today, in the remaining woodlands along the shores of the Great Lakes, flying squirrels, owls, porcupines and bats roost in white pines. Woodpeckers and beavers excavate different ends of the tree trunk, and songbirds perch in the forest canopy. White-tailed deer travel along riverside trails.

First Peoples

Earliest peoples hunted caribou and big game for food and clothing. As the climate warmed after the ice age, the culture and plants of the woodland people spread up from the south. Clay pots, tobacco pipes and copper arrived from native traders from the south. The Iroquoian-speaking Haudenosaunee dug up the rich soils to plant corn and lived in more permanent longhouses. (Haudenosaunee means "people building a long house.") They built villages on sites such as old volcanoes where they were safe from floods and could watch for enemies. They travelled along rivers in birch-bark canoes.

New Arrivals

In 1535, Jacques Cartier sailed up the St. Lawrence to the Haudenosaunee villages of Stadacona and Hochelaga. French fur traders and missionaries followed, and forts were constructed over deserted villages. French settlers built stone walls around their towns, and planted French crops in long rows down to the river. As the St. Lawrence River became more and more important for travel and trade, docks, canals and dams were built to improve shipping. Ottawa was born when the Rideau Canal was being dug to join the Ottawa River to Lake Ontario. Queen Victoria chose it as the capital of the colony in 1857. Railways began where the ships had to stop, such as at the La Chine rapids. Towns grew into cities as Canadian lumber, minerals and grain became important trading goods.

The Landscape Today

The Laurentian woodlands are rich with clues to 400 years of colonial settlement. From the citadel of Quebec City to Habitat, a space-age housing complex built for Expo 67 in Montreal, architectural landmarks have shaped the character of the cities. Over the centuries, dams and canals drastically changed the shape and ecosystems of the St. Lawrence River. Pollution from cities and factories continues to threaten the Great Lakes, and urban sprawl creeps over woodland habitat. Many species are at risk, such as the Atlantic salmon, the flying squirrel and the eastern bittern. But even in 1914, people knew that this unique region needed protection, so they established the St. Lawrence Islands National Park, Canada's smallest national park. Here species such as the red-headed woodpecker find refuge from development.

• **Why are farms along the St. Lawrence River so long and skinny?** Because when seigneurs (French lords) divided their lands for tenant farmers hundreds of years ago, each farm needed access to the river. To fit as many farms along the river as they could, they made them long and skinny.

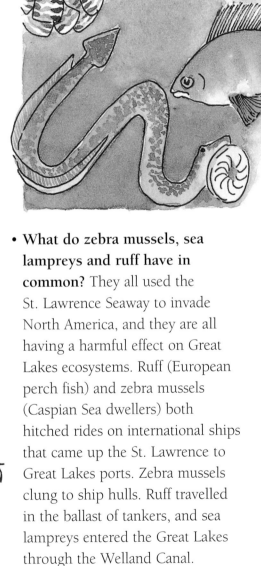

• **What does the peculiar star-nosed mole tell you about the Laurentian woodlands?** Known by its highly sensitive 22-tentacled nose, the star-nosed mole is able to detect insects in snow, ice, water and forest soil, all part of the woodland habitats from wetlands to snowy forest. This is the only mole in North America that has adapted to such a wide range of habitats.

• **What do zebra mussels, sea lampreys and ruff have in common?** They all used the St. Lawrence Seaway to invade North America, and they are all having a harmful effect on Great Lakes ecosystems. Ruff (European perch fish) and zebra mussels (Caspian Sea dwellers) both hitched rides on international ships that came up the St. Lawrence to Great Lakes ports. Zebra mussels clung to ship hulls. Ruff travelled in the ballast of tankers, and sea lampreys entered the Great Lakes through the Welland Canal.

• **Which of these three volcanoes isn't in the Laurentian woodlands: Mount St. Helens, Mount Royal or Mount Saint Hilaire?** Mount St. Helens is on the west coast of North America and erupted in 1980. Mount Royal (an urban park) and Mount Saint Hilaire (a biosphere reserve) are ancient extinct volcanoes in the Laurentians. Today, they offer a refuge for woodland plants and animals, such as jack-in-the-pulpits and monarch butterflies.

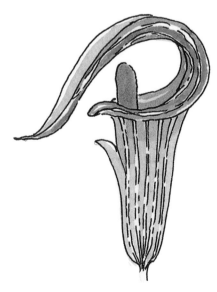

COASTAL RAIN FOREST

The mild, wet climate influenced by the Pacific Ocean makes this a place of wild, lush forests and rugged shorelines from isolated islands to deep fjords. It is one of the most biologically rich ecosystems on earth.

The Ancient Landscape

The rocky west coast and its islands are part of the last super-island to crash into the continent 70 million years ago. The crash created the Coast Mountains — the largest granite mass in the world. The edge of the continent is part of the Pacific Ring of Fire, where volcanoes still erupt and earthquakes rumble, causing tsunamis.

During the ice age, glaciers bulldozed valleys to the sea, but didn't reach all the islands and peninsulas. These places became refugia, like Banks Island. Ice sheets squished the south coast down making the north coast pop up creating the Hecate Plain. It sank back under the waves 8000 years ago. In the south, an inland sea was created, the Gulf of Georgia, which First Nations now call the Salish Sea. Deltas of fine sediments fanned out at river mouths in places such as the Fraser River delta.

Climate

Coastal shores and mountain slopes are buffeted year-round by ocean winds — making this the rainiest and windiest place in Canada and home of Canada's only rain forest. Rains pour down when clouds heavy with moisture are forced up the mountain slopes as they come in off the sea. On the other side of Vancouver Island's mountains, in the rain shadow of the Gulf of Georgia, summers are mild and dry, giving this smaller region a Mediterranean-like climate.

Rain forest

Rain shadow

Prince Rupert

Banks Island

Hecate Strait

Namu

Pacific Ocean

QUEEN CHARLOTTE ISLANDS

HAIDA GWAII

ALASKA

Ring of Fire

Pacific Ocean

COAST MOUNTAINS

Mt. Waddington

VANCOUVER ISLAND

Fraser River

Pacific Rim National Park

Vancouver

Victoria

Gulf of Georgia/ Salish Sea

USA

Plants and Animals

Craggy Sitka spruce trees colonized rocky shorelines because they could withstand saltwater spray. Western redcedar, salmonberries and devil's club moved into river floodplains about 7000 years ago. Swollen glacial rivers continue to cascade down valleys each spring. Trees rooted in nurse logs survive these huge flash floods.

The forest canopy is thick with mosses, lichens and small creatures. During the spawning season, bears and eagles feast on salmon, and fish remains fertilize forest plants. Woodpeckers excavate holes in trees, and owls and martens soon move in. The rain shadow region hosts Garry oak trees, camas flowers and Douglas-fir forests. Deer, elk and bear roam the grasslands and forest. In the ocean, plankton feed herring, and herring feed salmon, harbour seals and orcas.

First Peoples

Aboriginal peoples settled in estuaries and constructed stone fish traps to catch salmon. Some hunted whales from the sea. First Peoples on the coast spoke many different languages from Haida to Salish. Their connection with one another was by canoes made of redcedar. First Peoples used the "tree of life" to make clothing and medicines by stripping off its bark. You can find trees with strips torn off still growing in the forest today.

Salmon, whales and other animals were honoured in carvings on poles and rocks. These carvings and shell middens (places where shells were used for building foundations) mark village sites. The Salish-speaking people lived in the rain shadow of the Gulf of Georgia where they managed camas gardens such as potato fields and hunted deer and elk.

New Arrivals

Fur traders followed Captain Cook to the West Coast. They largely traded from their ships but left smallpox and seas empty of sea otters and then whales. When the gold rush and railway-building boom started in 1850, British traders started to build places such as Victoria that reminded them of England. Chinatowns sprung up to house the thousands of Chinese workers who provided goods and labour for gold rush towns, railways and logging camps. Forests of redcedar were cut for railway ties. When the gold ran out, immigrants came from Japan, India and Europe to farm the rich deltas and work in canneries up and down the coast. But declining fishing and logging industries forced people to find work in other places.

Today, most people live on the south coast around the Gulf of Georgia, near cities such as Victoria and Vancouver. The once vast Fraser delta supported huge flocks of migrating birds before much of it was farmed and later developed into the city and suburbs.

The Landscape Today

The last, largest, most intact temperate rain forest in the world is on the central and northern coast of British Columbia. Wolves, grizzly bears and whales still have enough habitat to live in these northern regions and waters. Coastal communities are turning more and more to ecotourism as people come from around the world to see the rain forest. And First Nations people have retained their distinctive ways of life centred around the sea.

Although the original Douglas-fir forests in the south are mostly gone, some redcedar and Sitka spruce rain forests along the outer coast of Vancouver Island are protected. If you hike through Pacific Rim National Park in Clayoquot Sound, you can visit these giant trees up close. In the Fraser River delta, the South Arm and Ladner marshes are protected stopovers for winged visitors travelling the Pacific flyway.

Spirit bears attract visitors from around the world.

The ancient village site of Namu was a cannery for a while.

• **What does the abandoned cannery at Namu tell you?** That less than 40 years ago Namu was a bustling fishing port where many people worked canning salmon and herring. Today, cruise-ship tourists snap pictures of the derelict cannery sliding into the sea. But under its rotting timbers lies another clue to British Columbia's coastal history. Here is an archaeological site that tells us early peoples started living here 10 000 years ago.

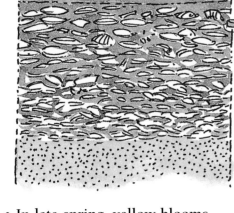

• **When you hike along the Trans-Canada Trail in the Cowichan Valley, why do some of the tree stumps look like faces with square eyes?** The notches were used to support two springboards, which loggers stood on to cut down huge Douglas-firs using only a crosscut saw. This saw needed two strong men to push and pull it through the old-growth trees that were as big around as a double-decker bus.

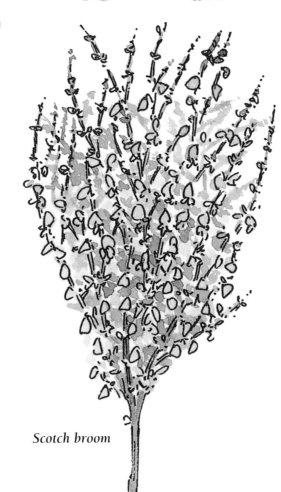

• **In late spring, yellow blooms appear all over southern Vancouver Island. Just another native plant enjoying the warm, sunny weather?** No, Scotch broom is an invasive plant that alters the soil and crowds out native species. But, like English ivy or Himalayan blackberry it is a clue to the people who settled here and planted gardens filled with plants from their British homeland.

Scotch broom

• **What do Prince Rupert, the Queen Charlotte Islands and Victoria all have in common?** They are all named after members of royal families who never visited the coastal rain forest. First Peoples had different names for these places. The Tsimshian people called the Prince Rupert area Laxspa'ws, meaning "island of sand." The Queen Charlotte Islands were known as Haida Gwaii — place of the Haida people. And the Salish-speaking Songhees people called the Victoria area Camosun, named after a waterfall there.

WESTERN CORDILLERA

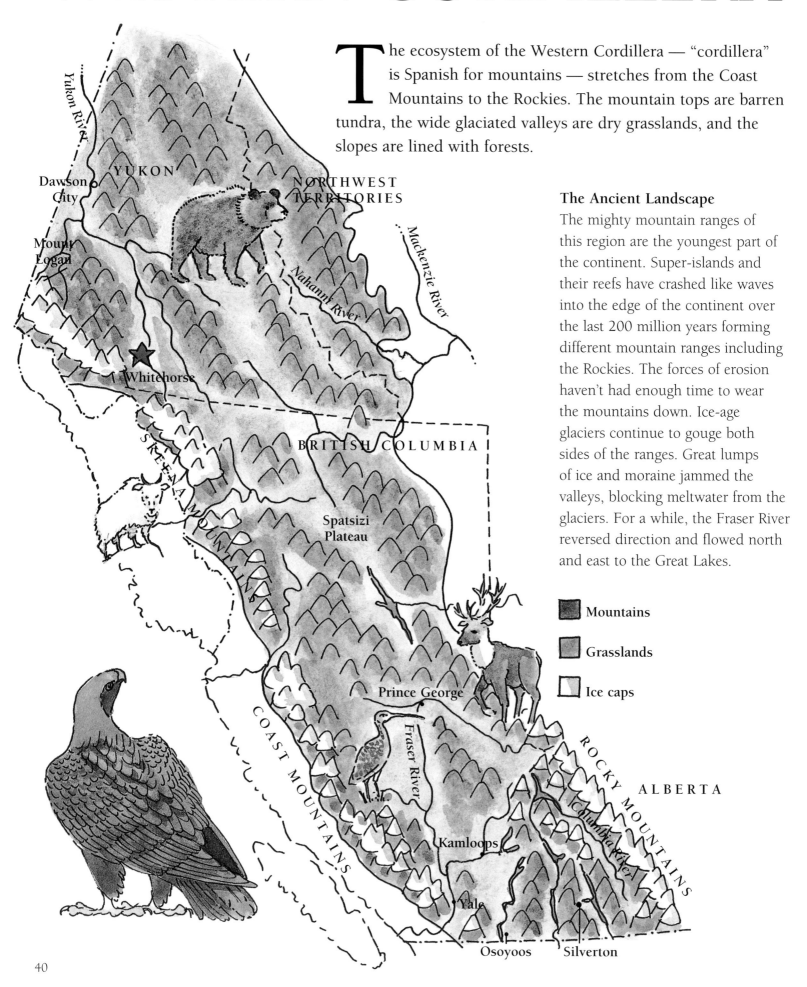

The ecosystem of the Western Cordillera — "cordillera" is Spanish for mountains — stretches from the Coast Mountains to the Rockies. The mountain tops are barren tundra, the wide glaciated valleys are dry grasslands, and the slopes are lined with forests.

The Ancient Landscape

The mighty mountain ranges of this region are the youngest part of the continent. Super-islands and their reefs have crashed like waves into the edge of the continent over the last 200 million years forming different mountain ranges including the Rockies. The forces of erosion haven't had enough time to wear the mountains down. Ice-age glaciers continue to gouge both sides of the ranges. Great lumps of ice and moraine jammed the valleys, blocking meltwater from the glaciers. For a while, the Fraser River reversed direction and flowed north and east to the Great Lakes.

Mountains

Grasslands

Ice caps

Climate

The Western Cordillera region has every climatic zone in Canada, from very dry to very cold. The elevation (the height something is above sea level) determines climate in this region. So the higher up you go, the colder it gets. Tall mountain peaks, even in southern Canada, are capped in ice, still in the grip of ice-age glaciers. The deep valleys and eastern slopes are in rain shadows. In the south, valleys widen into dry plateaus with sparse vegetation and strange, wind-shaped rocks. Osoyoos has the only pocket desert in Canada.

Plants and Animals

You can find everything from desert plants such as cactus to tundra species such as heather in the mountains. At high elevations, where it is too cold for trees to grow, flowering alpine meadows of lupins, paintbrushes and avalanche lilies flourish. If you lie on a ridge, you might spot golden eagles hunting pikas and marmots, while mountain goats watch from cliffs. At the treeline, in the southern mountains, Clark's nutcrackers feed on white-bark pine cones. Ptarmigan, which turn white in the winter, keep warm under the snowpack.

At lower elevations, the temperature warms. Here the subalpine forests of Engelmann spruce and subalpine fir grow, providing food for mountain caribou. Mule deer, elk, wolves and grizzlies migrate from the pine grasslands in the valleys up to the rain forests on the slopes.

First Peoples

As the ice sheets melted, families settled along rivers where deer, fish and freshwater mussels were plentiful. In winter, they hunted elk and mountain goats in the high country. They set the grassland valleys and plateaus on fire to keep them free of trees so the animals they hunted could graze. The Secwepemc-speakers built trails to the coast so they could trade for fish oils. The Kutenai-speakers hunted deer, elk and caribou in the interior plateau, and trailblazed to the Prairies to hunt bison. Their knowledge of mountain passes helped explorers find the west coast and, later, surveyors find a route for the Canadian Pacific Railway. In the northern mountains, the Athabaskan-speaking people forged trails between high and low country.

New Arrivals

With the discovery of gold in the western cordillera in 1858, the mountains suddenly were opened up to exploration by prospectors. Boomtowns such as Yale, Silverton and Dawson City were constructed overnight. You can still find traces of old tunnels and mine tailings (the waste left behind after panning for gold). Many unlucky prospectors turned to cattle ranching or farming in the foothills, plateaus and valleys. The forest slopes supplied them with timber and summer range for their animals. In the floodplains of big rivers such as the Columbia, they planted hay to feed their cattle. With the arrival of Canadian Pacific Railway in 1885, the cordillera also became a popular place for tourists, especially when Canada's first national park was established at Banff in 1885.

The Landscape Today

Mountain paintings of early twentieth century artists look a lot like what you'd see in the Western Cordillera today. But if you look closer, you'll see many changes. Glaciers have shrunk because the climate is changing. Dams to make electricity have changed river ecosystems and created new lakes. Where trading routes and game trails once ran are highways, towns, ranches and resorts. Golf courses dot valley bottoms.

When First Peoples could no longer burn grasslands, this important ecosystem began to fill in with trees. All these changes have altered the migration and feeding habits of wildlife. And some animals, such as the mountain caribou, are now endangered. But many people are working to preserve habitat and make wildlife corridors so animals can move safely from one area to another. And park wardens and First Nations are bringing back burning to help restore the grassland ecosystem.

- **If you see steam coming out of the ground, what does that tell you about your landscape?** That you're near a hot spring and an active volcanic hot spot. Hot springs occur when underground water is heated up by magma and bubbles to the surface. This water is often full of sulphur, so it's no mystery how Sulphur Mountain — home to Banff and its famous hot springs — got its name.

How does a hotspring work?

Cold water

Hot spring

Fault

Fault

Limestone

Magma

- **Why are there circular pits on the flat gravel benches above river valleys?** First Peoples dug pits and covered them with logs and sod to make insulated houses for the winter. They scooped out the gravel left by glaciers and rivers because it was easy to dig. You can visit a reconstructed pit house today at the Secwepemc Museum in Kamloops, BC.

- **What clue does the place name Spatsizi Plateau give you about this amazing home to the Tahltan people?** Spatsizi means "red goat" to the First People of this region. Mountain goats roll in the dust that comes off the red sandstone mountain at the headwaters of the Spatsizi River. The sandstone comes from ancient seabeds on which mountain goats now play.

- **Why are the spectacular features of the cordillera full of French names?** European geographers first named glacial features from observing the French Alps. When they came to describe Canada's mountains for geography books, they used the same names, such as arêtes (razor-sharp ridges separating two glacial valleys), roche moutonnée (sheep-shaped rocks formed by ice flowing over them), and cirques (small circular lakes scoured by glaciers).

PRAIRIE

The prairie ecosystem covers southern Alberta, Saskatchewan and Manitoba. The original Prairie was grasslands with groves of aspen growing along its northern edge.

The Ancient Landscape

By 75 million years ago, erosion had shaped the prairie landscape into a big, flat basin. Seas flooded in and dinosaurs sloshed through warm shallow lagoons and swamps. Decaying animals and plants became trapped in the layers of mud, sand and coral reefs, which became shale, sandstone and limestone. Over millions of years, and under much pressure, this once living matter turned into oil and gas. In deeper sea waters, mud and sand formed layers of shale and sandstone.

Moraine from ice-age glaciers butted up against hills and plugged up meltwater lakes, such as Lake Agassiz. When the plugs burst, spectacular flood waters ripped the till away, formed coulees, and exposed ancient seabeds. Ice chunks melted forming kettle lakes.

Tall grass prairie

Short grass prairie

Aspen groves

Edmonton • Vegreville North Saskatchewan River

Calgary • Herschel • Saskatoon

Last Mountain Lake

South Saskatchewan River Qu'Appelle River

Sand Hills Moose Mountain

Regina Assiniboine River

• Lethbridge S A S K A T C H E W A N

A L B E R T A Cypress Hills M A N I T O B A

□ Grasslands National Park

Climate

The prairie grasslands have a continental climate. Because of the rain shadow effect of the Western Cordillera, they are one of the driest areas of Canada. Summer brings hot temperatures and the threat of droughts, tornadoes, hail and thunderstorms. In winter, the Prairie receives snow and has some of the coldest temperatures on earth. But sometimes warm, dry winds, called chinooks, sweep off the Rockies and melt the snow in the western prairies.

Plants and Animals

Today, there are only a few areas where native grasses and wildflowers still grow. But for thousands of years, tall-grass prairie built up the rich, black soils of southern Manitoba and fed grazers such as bison, elk and pronghorn antelope. Predators such as the plains grizzlies and wolves thrived. Short-grass prairie grew in the drier southwest. Look closely at native prairie plants, such as bluestem bunchgrasses or pussytoes, and you'll find big roots or special hairy features that help them trap water and survive drought.

Animals such as swift foxes, burrowing owls, badgers and black-footed ferrets survived on the treeless grasslands by burrowing underground. Many birds of prey hunted and nested on the vast plains, and migratory birds stopped over in the wetlands of Manitoba. In the areas between prairie and boreal forest, aspen parklands took root.

First Peoples

To hunt bison, First Peoples had to move with the big grazers across the vast grasslands. Many groups roamed over the plains, competing for this important food source. Today, if you uncover an arrowhead, it might be from a battle or an ancient hunting site. If you stumble across a stone bison trap or a rock carving, it was probably made by the Assiniboine, an early plains people. Algonkian-speaking people and others from the south also lived on the Prairie at different times. Stone medicine wheels, such as the one at Moose Mountain, Saskatchewan, helped mark the seasonal rituals of the prairie dwellers.

Hawk's-eye view of a medicine wheel.

Winnipeg

Red River

New Arrivals

Many early fur traders married native women. These Métis families roamed the plains hunting buffalo and supplying pemmican to the trading forts. When the railway steamed in, hunting became easy and the bison were quickly eliminated. (There were 60 million bison in the 1700s in North America. A century later, there were less than a thousand.) The Prairies lost a key part of the ecosystem.

Surveyors divided up the Prairie into a checkerboard of farms, roads and settlements that were named by Scottish, Mennonite, Acadian and other immigrants. Each town built a grain elevator by the train tracks. Mormon settlers developed irrigation systems for farming on dry land, and British settlers took up cattle ranching. Ukrainians arrived and erected their onion-domed churches. Eventually, most of the native prairie was plowed and replaced with crops. Many settlers struggled with droughts, yearly floods or plagues of grasshoppers.

• **What does the giant Easter egg near Vegreville, Alberta, tell you?**
That this grassy landscape, with its rich dark earth, aspen woodlands and icy rivers drew Ukranian immigrants because it reminded them of the steppes they left behind in the Ukraine. Decorating Easter eggs, or *pysanka*, was a Ukrainian tradition they brought with them.

The Landscape Today

Today, the native grasslands are among the most endangered ecosystems in Canada. Species such as the black-footed ferret have been pushed into refugia such as Grasslands National Park, while other species, such as the grizzly bear, have disappeared. But coyotes and prairie gophers thrive because they have adapted to human settlements. Some Canadians have created wildlife sanctuaries with breeding programs to help save the swift fox and the whooping crane.

Disappearing grain elevators are a sign of more changes on the prairie landscape. Even train tracks have vanished. Many family farms have been turned into large-scale industrial farming operations, and many farm families have moved to the cities and suburbs. The prairies still remain the breadbasket of the world, but the diversity of grains has diminished.

• **What do fossils of magnolia plants tell you about the grasslands?** If you live near Val Marie, by Grasslands National Park, you can find fossils of magnolias. These were the earth's first flowering plants, making this place home to the ancestors of our food plants.

• **What can a big rock in the middle of the prairie tell you about Herschel, Saskatchewan?** Sitting in the middle of Herschel is an erratic left by the ice sheets. The Assinboine carved them to teach their children about the importance of bison to their way of life. On the same rock, you can trace the marks bison left behind when they scratched their horns on it.

• **What does bluestem bunchgrass tell you about the prairie landscape?** You can stomp and chomp it like a bison, burn it, deprive it of water for most of the year, then swamp it in a flood and it will still survive. Bluestem, with its massive root system, tells you that you are in an ecosystem of big grazers, fire, flood and drought. What bluestem can't survive is the plow. But at Last Mountain Lake in southern Saskatchewan, you can see a restored prairie.

• **Why was Winnipeg built around two rivers that flood regularly?** Winnipeg is a Cree word meaning "muddy water." It marks the place of an important trading junction of two famous rivers, the Red and the Assiniboine. First Peoples used these rivers as trading routes. So did the Hudson's Bay Company, founder of Fort Garry.

ACADIAN WOODLANDS

The Acadian woodlands is the ecosystem of the Maritimes. These are the craggy places where the southern woodlands, northern boreal forest and ocean meet. Although Newfoundland shares many aspects of maritime ecosystems and culture, the forests of this northern island are boreal.

The Ancient Landscape

When the continents were drifting around the globe, a piece of Africa glommed on to the east coast of Newfoundland, and old seabeds crumpled up into the Appalachian Mountains with the collision. Erosion wore down the mountains, and the sediments ran down the rivers to the continental shelf. After the glaciers melted, the sea sloshed into the Bay of Fundy. Nova Scotia was an island until land surfaced again and the bay shrank leaving fertile soils behind.

Climate

The foggy autumn days, cool summer breezes off the ocean and fierce winter storms have made the Maritimes a challenging environment to live in. The Labrador Current bringing icebergs and cold water down from the Arctic keeps summer temperatures cool and winters long. The Gulf Stream brings warm waters up from the Gulf of Mexico, which mix with the cold waters and cause wild storms.

Avalonia 600 million years ago

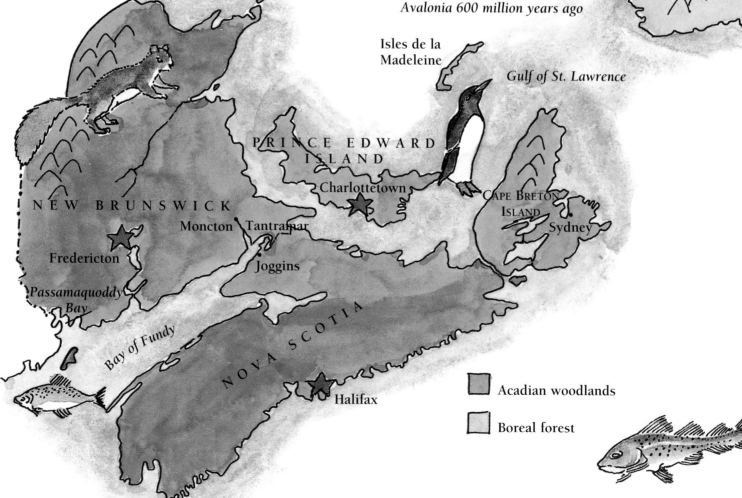

Plants and Animals

The cauldron of currents and tides makes this region one of the richest places in the world for marine creatures — from plankton and smelt to sperm whales and giant squids. Once it was the world's largest cod-breeding grounds and the home to 65 species of seabirds, including the great auk (now extinct) and 15 kinds of whales.

The blubber of whales, puffins, murres and gannets is a clue to the harsh environment they live in. The fat comes from oily fish such as herring and capelin. Atlantic salmon and sturgeon brought nutrients to forest creatures when they spawned up rivers. Spruce, pine and balsam fir mingled with hardwoods, creating a mixed woodland inhabited by many creatures — from grey squirrels and wolves to wood frogs and woodland caribou.

First Peoples

Net sinkers, harpoons and sculptures of marine life are clues that First Peoples fished from summer camps on the coast. They gathered food plants from the salt marshes and birds' eggs from the islands. To escape winter gales, they moved inland and set up skin tents to hunt caribou. People came from the southwest bringing the technology of pottery. You can still find bits of these pots today. Mysterious burial mounds and the remains of shallow pit houses hold stories of their daily life. And place names tell of ancient cultures, such as Passamaquoddy Bay, which in Algonkian means "place of lots of pollock" — an important food fish.

The descendants of the early people are the Algonkian-speaking Maliseet and Mi'kmaq people. They traded goods with French fur traders, but most died because of war, disease and starvation. The Beothuk people of Newfoundland were completely eliminated by war and disease.

L'Anse aux Meadows

Bonavista

NEWFOUNDLAND

Heart's Delight

St. John's

Avalon Peninsula

Fortune Bay

New Arrivals

Vikings settled briefly at L'Anse aux Meadows in Newfoundland 1000 years ago. Across the Strait of Belle Isle, Basque whalers built their camp just over 500 years later. Europeans fished the Grand Banks, some settling in fishing villages with names they borrowed from home, such as New Glasgow. Many marine species, such as the walrus, were hunted out. And the great auk was hunted to extinction by 1844.

French farmers settled around the Bay of Fundy, calling the country Acadia. Dykes in the salt marshes are clues that the Acadians farmed these fertile soils before the British deported them to other colonies. The ancient forests, like you see as fossilized forests at Joggins, became the coal mines of Cape Breton. Loyalists from the United States, and later, black slaves, moved here to escape persecution.

The Landscape Today

There are few original Acadian woodlands left today. The fertile lowlands were cleared for farms and orchards. The upland forests stocked the busy shipyards of Halifax with wood to build tall ships. The wolf, cougar and woodland caribou, which lived in the forest, were hunted out, and the ecosystem lost important providers of nutrients to the soil. But many Canadians are trying to restore ancient woodlands by reintroducing species that have disappeared, such as the fisher and the peregrine falcon.

Today on the coast, tourists shoot whales and seabirds with cameras, not guns, and view wildlife from protected areas such as Fundy National Park. Visitors can also go down coal mines, visit Acadian barns, wander in fishing villages and walk along railway lines converted into the Trans-Canada Trail.

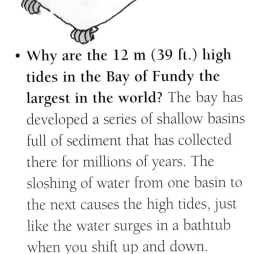

• **What do music, trees and old boats have in common?** They all come together to make Acadian fiddles sing. For hundreds of years, wood from maple trees and white pines was used to make fiddles, boats and the wharves to which the boats tied up. Famous schooners, such as the *Bluenose* on the Canadian dime, and the wharves they were tied up to, were built from huge trees, which

are rarely found now. The trees were cut at a time when Maritime shipbuilders were the best in the world. The sleek vessels speeded up trade across the Atlantic. Maritimers wrote songs about the boats, the sailing life and the beauty of the maple trees.

• **What and where is Bonavista?** In the famous Newfoundland song "I'se the bye that catches the fish" the boy or fisherman goes to fish at Bonavista, a peninsula that juts out into the Atlantic Ocean. "Bona Vista" means "happy sight" in Italian and is where Italian explorer John Cabot first stepped ashore in the new world. It now has a famous lighthouse on it.

• **Why are the 12 m (39 ft.) high tides in the Bay of Fundy the largest in the world?** The bay has developed a series of shallow basins full of sediment that has collected there for millions of years. The sloshing of water from one basin to the next causes the high tides, just like the water surges in a bathtub when you shift up and down.

• **From the name alone, how would you know that the Tantramar marshes near Sackville, New Brunswick, are an important stopping place for migrating birds?** In French, "tantramar" refers to the loud noise of water birds on the marsh. Plovers, sandpipers, ducks and geese visit this area on their way to breeding grounds. Early settlers wrote that the sky turned black because there were so many birds.

CAROLINIAN WOODLANDS

The Carolinian woodlands are in the southern triangle of land cradled by the Great Lakes. Because it is so warm and humid, this ecosystem resembles the almost tropical woodlands of the Carolinas in the United States — giving this ecosystem its name.

The Ancient Landscape

A billion years ago, the North American and African plates shifted and ripped open the belly of North America, creating a basin for the Great Lakes. Over 300 million years ago, a sea flooded in and left layers of sand, shells and clay that turned into limestone and shale. When the glaciers bulldozed the region, the soft layers of shale crumbled and left harder limestone jutting up, such as the Niagara Escarpment and Falls.

Lake levels rose and fell and left behind rich soils of silt and clay.

Climate

In this flat, small triangle, summers are the hottest, longest and most humid in Canada. Surrounded on three sides by the world's largest freshwater system, the Great Lakes, this tiny corner of the country feels subtropical in summer.

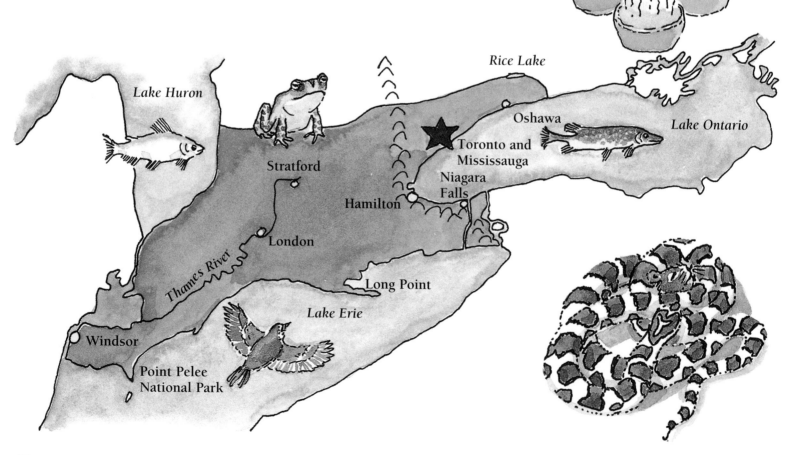

Plants and Animals

The Great Lakes surrounding this region formed the largest, richest, freshwater ecosystem in the world (nearly 250 000 km²). Lots of water and hot summers attracted a huge diversity of plants and animals. Beavers gnawed mazes through the wetlands. Exotic tulip trees, sassafras and spice bushes grew among stately beeches and oaks. At one time, the woodlands were so dense that flying squirrels could soar from tree to tree all the way from Oshawa to Windsor. Canada's largest snakes and hundreds of songbirds, such as the hooded warbler, migrated through here. The rich soils and long growing season attracted farmers who planted fruit trees and grapevines in places such as the Niagara Peninsula.

First Peoples

The woodlands people, who left behind pottery remains, travelled lightly on the landscape. Over time, a farming culture evolved. The Neutrals shaped the land by clearing it for cornfields and longhouse settlements. During a war with other Iroquoian-speaking tribes, the Neutrals were driven out of their homes. For the next 300 years, the Haudenosaunee farmed and hunted beaver on the land.

When the beaver were wiped out during fur-trading days, a whole of way life disappeared.

New Arrivals

Surveyors divided the land of this region into 200 acre (81 ha) farms for the Loyalists from the United States who arrived in the late 1700s. The surveyors laid out market towns 19 km (12 mi.) apart so people could travel from their farms in a day. Immigrants flocked to this area because it was the most fertile place in Canada. They planted wheat and vegetables on the silt and clay soils. On sandy soil, they grew tobacco, a native plant in this region. Each farming family maintained a woodlot to supply firewood. They called this land the "back 40," referring to its size — 40 acres (16 ha).

Fishing towns dotted the shores of Lakes Ontario, Erie and Huron so people could harvest whitefish and lake trout. Factories also grew up along these shores, especially after the St. Lawrence Seaway opened up shipping from the Atlantic. Ports such as Toronto turned into big cities, and suburbs started to spread over the land.

The Landscape Today

Today, this region is the most populated part of Canada. The only patches of Carolinian woodland left are the last of the "back 40s," pioneer graveyards and protected areas such as Point Pelee National Park. Silos, barns and water towers, which stood where pines and oaks once grew, are giving way to industrial parks and strip malls. Skyscrapers tower over ancient Haudenosaunee fields, and freeways and suburbs cover beaver wetlands. The only clues to the huge fishing industry of the Great Lakes are old wharves in places such as Port Dover. Overfishing, pollution and invasive species, such as the sea lamprey, have contributed to the decline of native species such as lake trout in Lake Erie. This ecoregion is the most endangered and threatened place in Canada, but many people are working to restore the few woodland areas left, such as those around Long Point.

- **Where can you walk along a wooden railway trestle and look down onto an ancient seabed?**
Hiking along the Bruce Trail, following the Niagara Escarpment, home of Niagara Falls. This 800 km (500 mi.) corridor along abandoned railway beds, canal locks, and aboriginal hunting trails threads its way past caves, quarries, waterfalls and ridges through millions of years of history. It is Canada's oldest and longest hiking trail.

- **Why do barns on the sandy shores of Lake Erie have lots of vents in their roofs?** These vents help air get in to dry tobacco. Tobacco is a native North American plant that was grown by the Haudenosaunee for medicine and sacred rituals. It flourishes on the sandy soils of old lakeshores and was one of the trade goods that excited Europeans, such as Sir Walter Raleigh, in North America. The tobacco-growing industry in this area is now slowing down as smoking declines. Many farmers have turned to growing other cash crops such as ginseng that thrive in the sandy soil.

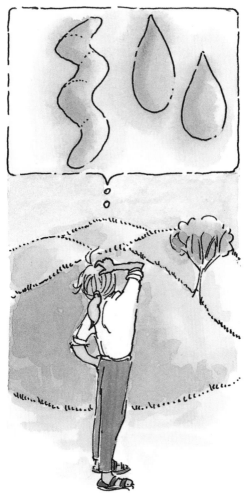

- **What's the connection between ice-age mastodons and tulip trees?** Mastodons stripped tulip trees with the help of their trunks and spread the seeds in their droppings, which helped them germinate. Today, no other animals eat and distribute the large fruit of these trees. And even if they did, there isn't much habitat left for these plants to grow in. Biosphere reserves such as Long Point Provincial Park, and even your backyards, are like Jurassic Parks — refugia, for these ancient trees. The mastodons have long gone.

- **What are the strange mounds in this region and how did they form?**
There are two strange mounds you might stumble across in a Carolinian woodland: straight mounds and S-shaped mounds. Straight mounds are drumlins deposited by glaciers. Churches were often built on drumlins so that all the surrounding farms could see them. S-shaped mounds, such as the Serpent Mount of Rice Lake, are sacred burial mounds built by early woodlands people.

INDEX